WRITING TO EXPLAIN

REPRODUCIBLE LESSONS

by

Kathleen A. Rogers

Fearon Teacher Aids
Torrance, California
A Division of Frank Schaffer Publications, Inc.

Illustrator: Bradley Dutsch

This Fearon Teachers Aids product was formerly manufactured and distributed by American Teaching Aids, Inc., a subsidiary of Silver Burdett Ginn, and is now manufactured and distributed by Frank Schaffer Publications, Inc. FEARON, FEARON TEACHER AIDS and the FEARON balloon logo are marks used under license from Simon & Schuster, Inc.

ISBN 0-8224-7537-5

Printed in the United States of America.

1. 9   8   7   6   5   4

CONTENTS

CONTENTS (Continued)

Completing Comparison/Contrast Sentences

Comparison sentences show how two ideas are alike. Contrast sentences show how two ideas are different. Ideas that are alike or different can be combined into one sentence by connecting the ideas with signal words.

| Comparison Signal Words: also, as, compare, contrast, same | Contrast Signal Words: although, but, however, on the other hand, yet |

Directions: First circle the signal word in each sentence. Then complete the sentence. The first one has been done for you.

1. The movie was filled with adventure, (but) **I thought it was boring.** _____

2. Although the electricity went out, _____

_____

3. The children were terrified of ghosts; yet, _____

_____

4. My sister and I are very similar, but _____

_____

5. I would love to visit Disneyland; on the other hand, _____

_____

6. Fluoride in water helps prevent cavities, just as _____

_____

7. Jeff always comes late; however, _____

_____

8. It was Saturday morning, but _____

_____

9. I like my younger brother; also, _____

_____

10. Baseball is my favorite sport; on the other hand, _____

_____

Name _____

Combining Comparison/Contrast Sentences

You know that comparison sentences point out likenesses with words such as **also, as,** and **same.** You know, too, that contrast sentences use words like **although, but,** and **yet** to point out differences. Combine each of the following two sentences into one good comparison/contrast sentence. Remember to use the signal words listed on page 1.

1. The storm dumped fifteen inches of snow in the town north of us. We got five inches.

   _____

   _____

2. The Iroquois Indians built their houses from birch trees and young saplings. The Plains Indians preferred to use the hides of buffaloes for their shelters.

   _____

   _____

3. The twins look exactly alike. They have different personalities.

   _____

   _____

4. My mother has curly black hair. I have curly black hair.

   _____

   _____

5. Fruits are good for your health. Vegetables are good for you.

   _____

   _____

6. It was cold inside the house. It was cold outside.

   _____

   _____

Completing Cause/Result Sentences

A cause sentence gives the reason an event or action happened. A result sentence shows the consequence or effect of an action or event. Sentences that show cause and result can be combined by connecting the ideas with signal words.

Cause Signal Words: because, for the reason, similar, the cause	Result Signal Words: as a result, consequently, therefore, thus

Directions: First circle the signal word in each sentence. Then complete the sentence. The first sentence has been done for you.

1.   My cat is finicky; (therefore) **he will only eat the food we eat.** _____

2.   The reason the outfielder dropped the ball was _____

_____

3.   The storm knocked down our power line; thus, _____

_____

4.   Because the driver did not see the red traffic light, _____

_____

5.   My dog scares the mail carrier; as a result, _____

_____

6.   Our school bus broke down; therefore, _____

_____

Combining Cause/Result Sentences

Combine each set of sentences into one sentence that shows cause/result. Remember to use signal words.

Cause Signal Words: because, for the reason, similar, the cause	Result Signal Words: as a result, consequently, therefore, thus

1. My brother sleeps with an open book under his pillow. He says it helps him learn his lesson.

   _____

   _____

2. The groundhog saw its shadow. We will have six more weeks of winter.

   _____

   _____

3. The radio play *War of the Worlds* frightened many listeners. They thought it was a real Martian invasion.

   _____

   _____

4. Our school's air conditioner wasn't working right. We didn't have classes for three days.

   _____

   _____

5. My sister wasn't watching where she was going. She stepped on the cat's tail.

   _____

   _____

6. My brother studies very hard. He always makes the honor roll.

   _____

   _____

Writing to Explain copyright © 1987

Name _____

Using Examples

We can use examples to help make our ideas clear to the reader. Below are several statements. Write an example that explains each one. Be sure to write in complete sentences. The first one has been done for you.

1. Skating on thin ice can be dangerous. For instance, **last year my friend fell through thin ice and nearly drowned. Luckily a man pulled her out.**

2. Baby sisters and brothers are cute, but they can also be pests. For example, _____ _____ _____ _____

3. Writing a good paragraph takes a lot of time. _____ _____ _____ _____

4. There is always confusion at our dinner table. _____ _____ _____ _____

5. My brother cannot live without TV. _____ _____ _____ _____

Name _____

Writing with Examples

One way to develop an idea in a paragraph is to give examples that explain the topic sentence. To make the paragraph more interesting, add details and facts about each example.

Directions: Read the following paragraph. Circle each example, and underline specific details that explain each example.

Topic Sentence: <u>Many animals are smart</u>. A dog, for instance, can be trained to do many things. Some are taught to do police work. Some are trained to find people lost in the mountains. Seeing Eye dogs guide blind people safely through their daily tasks. Although many people don't realize it, pigs are also quite smart. They can learn to do many things. One pig even starred in a television series. Everyone knows chimpanzees are smart. Some chimps can use sign language and even spell simple words.

Directions: Now write your own example/detail paragraph. Include at least four examples in your paragraph. Add details to explain each example.

Topic Sentence: The ice cream flavor I buy depends upon my mood. _____

_____

_____

_____

_____

_____

_____

_____

_____

_____

_____

Writing to Explain copyright © 1987

Writing Definitions I

When writing explanatory paragraphs sometimes you must explain or define a word. A clear definition should include three parts:

1. what the word means,
2. a description or list of special traits,
3. an example.

Example: **Actor**

           meaning   **description**
An actor is a person who plays a part. He makes you believe he is someone else.
                    example
Sylvester Stallone is an actor who really makes you think he is Rocky, the champion boxer.

Directions: Write clear definitions for each of the following words. The words on this page have been partially done for you. You may use a dictionary for help.

igloo

1. An igloo is a _____ that _____
_____ . Eskimos used to live in igloos.

explorer

2. An explorer is a _____ who _____
_____ . An example of a famous explorer
is _____ , who discovered _____ .

fearful

Fearful is a _____ . When a person is fearful, he or she
_____ . _____
_____ is an example of a
fearful situation.

Writing Definitions II

Write sentences that explain the following words. Your definitions should include the meaning, a description, and an example. You may use a dictionary for help.

arithmetic

1. Arithmetic _____

_____

_____

superstition

2. A superstition _____

_____

_____

the United States

3. The United States _____

_____

_____

bicycle

4. A bicycle _____

_____

_____

transportation

5. Transportation _____

_____

_____

Describing the Contents of a Time Capsule

Zed Starflight lives in the year 2262. While building an Interstellar Launch Pad in his backyard, he discovered a time capsule that had been buried there in the year 1986.

Pretend you are Zed and describe three things you found in the capsule. Before you begin, remember:

1. that you must describe a real invention or gadget;
2. that you live in the twenty-third century, and that you may not be sure what the gadget is, or how it is used.

Describe the objects you found in the chart below.

	Object 1	Object 2	Object 3
size			
shape			
unusual markings			
color			
material made of			
what it looks like			
possible uses			

Explaining Observations

Using the information you wrote on page 9, write a paragraph describing the discovery of the time capsule and its contents. Be sure to include the observations you made on your chart.

    The other day while I was digging the foundation for a launch pad in my backyard, I made a most unusual discovery. _____

_____

_____

_____

_____

_____

_____

_____

_____

_____

_____

_____

_____

_____

_____

_____

_____

_____

Writing Introductory Paragraphs I

An introductory paragraph does two things. It catches the interest of the reader and it briefly tells the reader about the topic. One way to begin an introductory paragraph is to ask a question and then answer it. The answer should include details that will both interest and introduce the reader to your topic. Look at the following example.

topic: Planning a Surprise Party

opening question: Have you ever planned a surprise party? If you haven't, don't worry. It is easy to do. There are only four things you must do: (1) Keep

answers: the party a secret. (2) Use a place the guest won't suspect. (3) Get everyone to the party before the guest. (4) Use a foolproof plan for getting the guest to the party.

Directions: Choose one of the following topics and write an introductory paragraph using the question/answer style.

Topics: 1. How to make a scary Halloween costume
                  2. How to make friends
                  3. How to dress for a rock concert
                  4. What makes a good vacation

Topic # ____   _____

_____

_____

_____

_____

_____

_____

_____

_____

_____

_____

_____

_____

Name _____

Writing Introductory Paragraphs II

Another easy way to introduce the topic you want to write about is to use an anecdote in your first paragraph. An anecdote is an interesting or funny story about your topic. Here's an example:

topic: Planning a Surprise Party

interesting   The first surprise party I planned was a disaster! The party
or funny   was for my best friend Melinda. Her mom and I planned the party for
information: right after school. We had great snacks and a large chocolate cake
                         to eat. The house had been decorated with red and white streamers.
                         The only thing missing was Melinda. We didn't know it, but she had to
                         stay after school!

Directions: Write an introductory paragraph containing an anecdote that tells something
                interesting or funny about your topic. Use the same topic you chose for
                Writing Introductory Paragraphs I.

Topics: 1. How to make a scary Halloween costume
                2. How to make friends
                3. How to dress for a rock concert
                4. What makes a good vacation

Topic # ____   _____

_____

_____

_____

_____

_____

_____

_____

_____

_____

_____

Designing a New Gadget

Sticks stand straight and stiff, but springs bounce and coil. What could you make if you used the two together?

Step 1: Imagine a gadget you could make from springs and sticks. What would it look like? What other materials would you need? (Perhaps you would need rubber bands, string, paper clips, or boards.)

Step 2: Draw your gadget below.

Step 3: Explain your gadget.

1. What is it called? _____

2. What does it do? _____

_____

3. Describe its appearance. _____

_____

_____

_____

Describing a New Gadget

Using the notes you made on page 13, write a well-developed paragraph describing or explaining the new gadget you invented.

_____

_____

_____

_____

_____

_____

_____

_____

_____

_____

_____

_____

_____

_____

_____

_____

_____

_____

_____

_____

_____

_____

Writing an Autobiography

Directions: A person who writes about his or her own life writes an **autobiography.** You are to write a brief autobiography. Before you begin, jot down some important facts about yourself.

1. Where and when were you born? _____

   _____

2. Do you know anything interesting or funny about your birth or what you did as a baby?

   Explain. _____

   _____

   _____

3. Describe the way you look. Use adjectives and picture descriptions.
   Example: I have shiny, dark hair with curls so tight they bounce when I walk.

   hair _____

   eyes _____

   nose _____

   height and weight _____

4. List three words that best describe your personality. Give an example to support each word.

   a. _____

   _____

   b. _____

   _____

   c. _____

   _____

Writing an Autobiography

5. List the three most important or exciting events in your life. Explain each briefly.

a. _____

_____

_____

b. _____

_____

_____

c. _____

_____

_____

6. What else would you like to include about yourself? Write your ideas below. You might consider favorite hobbies, things you like, things you dislike, and your family.

_____

_____

_____

_____

_____

_____

_____

_____

_____

_____

Now you are ready to write your autobiography. Write it on a separate sheet of paper. Be sure to include the information covered in the six sections of your outline.

Writing to Explain copyright © 1987

Explaining the Use of an Object

An ordinary stick can be used in many ways. For example, it can be used to build fires, to beat a drum, or to catch a fish.

Step 1: Now think of two or three uses for a pencil.

Step 2: On the lines below, write a well-developed paragraph describing two or three different uses for a pencil.

_____

_____

_____

_____

_____

_____

_____

_____

_____

_____

_____

_____

_____

_____

_____

_____

_____

_____

Writing to Explain

Your class has a substitute teacher, and you have been chosen to be the substitute's "Teacher Aide" for the day. Your first job is to explain clearly the opening duties for the class. Then go on to list the subjects to be taught and the activities that each class period will cover. Write this information below. You may need to continue your list on a separate piece of paper.

_____

_____

_____

_____

_____

_____

_____

_____

_____

_____

_____

_____

_____

_____

_____

_____

_____

_____

_____

Writing to Explain copyright © 1987

Name _____

Comparing and Contrasting Two Articles

When you look at a sneaker and a boot, you can see that they differ in many ways. Write at least three ways in which they are different.

Sneaker	Boot
1. _____	1. _____
2. _____	2. _____
3. _____	3. _____

Of course, a sneaker and a boot are similar, too. Write at least three ways in which they are alike.

1. _____

2. _____

3. _____

A television and a stereo are also different. Write at least three ways in which they are different.

Television	Stereo
1. _____	1. _____
2. _____	2. _____
3. _____	3. _____

If you think carefully, you will think of many ways a television and a stereo are the same. Write three ways in which they are alike.

1. _____

2. _____

3. _____

Name _____

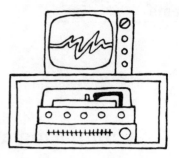

Writing to Compare and Contrast Two Articles

Using the information you wrote on page 19, write a paragraph comparing and contrasting the sneaker and the boot *or* the television and the stereo. Try to use at least four signal words in your paragraph.

> Signal Words: alike, also, different, however, in comparison, in contrast, on the other hand, similar

_____

_____

_____

_____

_____

_____

_____

_____

_____

_____

_____

_____

_____

_____

_____

_____

_____

Comparing and Contrasting Two People

Step 1: In the space below, compare and contrast yourself with another person you know well. This person could be a friend, a relative, or a neighbor.

Step 2: Think of specific details, situations, or events that illustrate each similarity or difference.

I will compare and contrast myself with _____ .

Ways we are alike:

1. _____

_____

2. _____

_____

3. _____

_____

Ways we are different:

1. _____

_____

_____

2. _____

_____

_____

3. _____

_____

_____

Name _____

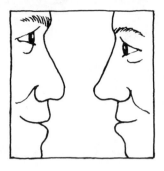

Writing to Compare and Contrast Two People

Using the notes you made on page 21, write two paragraphs showing how you are alike and how you are different from the person you are comparing yourself with. In your paragraphs try to use at least four signal words.

Comparison/Contrast Signal Words:

    alike, also, but, different, however, in contrast,
    on the other hand, resemble, same as, similar

_____

_____

_____

_____

_____

_____

_____

_____

_____

_____

_____

_____

_____

_____

_____

_____

_____

_____

Name _____

Comparing and Contrasting Two Creatures

There are many tales about mysterious half-human/half-animal creatures who wander the earth in wilderness areas. Below are some observations about the Abominable Snowman and Bigfoot.

Abominable Snowman	Bigfoot
ape-like man	ape-like man
shaggy reddish-brown hair over body	dark brown or black hair over body
about 6½′ tall	over 6½′ tall, some say 8′ tall
footprints 13″ long	footprints 16″ long
usually seen alone or with one other creature	usually seen alone, but stories say whole families exist
eats goats and vegetables	eats roots, berries, and leaves in summer and meat in winter
located in Himalayan Mountain areas	located primarily in Pacific Northwest wilderness

Directions: Regroup these statements by likenesses and differences.

Likenesses

1. _____

2. _____

3. _____

Differences

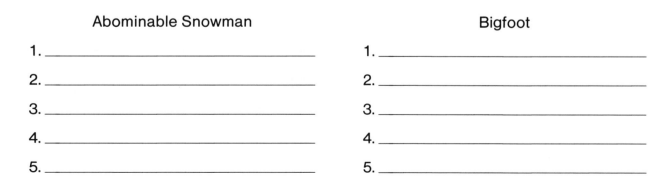

Abominable Snowman

1. _____

2. _____

3. _____

4. _____

5. _____

Bigfoot

1. _____

2. _____

3. _____

4. _____

5. _____

Writing to Explain copyright © 1987

Writing to Compare and Contrast Two Creatures

Write two paragraphs about the Abominable Snowman and Bigfoot. In the first paragraph discuss their likenesses, and in the second paragraph discuss their differences. Remember to use comparison/contrast signal words.

Comparison/Contrast Signal Words:

alike, also, but, different, however, in contrast, on the other hand, resemble, same as, similar

_____

_____

_____

_____

_____

_____

_____

_____

_____

_____

_____

_____

_____

_____

_____

_____

_____

Writing to Explain copyright © 1987

Name _____

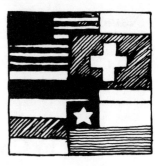

Comparing and Contrasting in Social Studies

The ability to make comparisons and contrasts is important in social studies. Often you are asked to write about the similarities and differences among people and places you have read about. The writers of the books you read use words such as **alike, also, but, different, however,** and **similar** to signal comparisons and contrasts.

Choose two groups of people, two countries, or two states and then fill out the comparison/contrast chart below. You may use your social studies textbook or some other source for getting information, if you need to.

I will compare and contrast _____ with _____ .

Four ways they are alike:

1. _____   3. _____

_____   _____

2. _____   4. _____

_____   _____

Four ways they are different:

1. _____   1. _____

_____   _____

2. _____   2. _____

_____   _____

3. _____   3. _____

_____   _____

4. _____   4. _____

_____   _____

Writing to Compare and Contrast in Social Studies

Write two paragraphs showing how the topics you chose on page 25 are alike and how they are different from one another. Remember to use signal words in your sentences.

Comparison/Contrast Signal Words:

alike, also, but, different, however, in contrast,
on the other hand, resemble, same as, similar

_____

_____

_____

_____

_____

_____

_____

_____

_____

_____

_____

_____

_____

_____

_____

_____

_____

_____

Inventing Solutions I

Every day each of us has to solve problems. From the time we get up in the morning until the time we go to bed at night, we decide things such as what to wear, what to eat, what to buy, and what to do in unexpected situations. Are you good at solving problems? Write two solutions to each of the following problems. Remember to write in complete sentences.

1. Problem: A heavy rainstorm begins on your way home from school. You rush home and discover that no one is home and you have lost your key.

Solution a: _____

_____

_____

_____

Solution b: _____

_____

_____

_____

2. Problem: When you were younger, you were chased by a big dog. Since then you have been terrified of all dogs. As you walk home from school, you see your neighbor's Doberman coming toward you. You look around for help, but no one is there.

Solution a: _____

_____

_____

_____

Solution b: _____

_____

_____

_____

Writing to Explain copyright © 1987

Name _____

Inventing Solutions II

Here are two more problems for you to solve. Present your solutions clearly and logically and in complete sentences.

1. Problem: Your mother, on her way to an important business meeting, drops you off at a party. Just as you get out of the car, you notice that everyone is wearing a costume except you.

Solution a: _____

_____

_____

_____

Solution b: _____

_____

_____

_____

2. Problem: You are sightseeing alone in a foreign city. The bicycle you rented breaks down. You have no money with you and you cannot speak the native language.

Solution a: _____

_____

_____

_____

Solution b: _____

_____

_____

_____

Writing to Explain copyright © 1987

Name _____

Defining a Problem

A paragraph that describes a problem should have three parts. It should tell:

1. what the problem is,
2. the cause(s) of the problem,
3. the effect(s) of the problem.

Step 1: Read the following paragraph.

Each year Mr. and Mrs. Cross and their children go on a family camping trip. Everyone in the family except Chris, the oldest child, loves the annual trip and looks forward to it. Chris hates camping and refuses to go anymore. Last year ants got into his sleeping bag and bit his legs. When he took his bag to a stream to wash out the ants, a strong current caught it and carried it away. On the third night in camp a stray dog came into their site and ran off with Chris's only pair of sneakers. Two days later Chris found another stray animal at the family campsite. It was black with a white stripe down its back. Before Chris could move away, the frightened skunk fired its spray. Chris's clothes, including his favorite T-shirt, had to be thrown away. No one wanted to get near him, either! Chris resolved never to go camping again. But the next family trip is coming up in two weeks, and his family is as determined to go as he is not to.

Step 2: Identify the three problem parts of the above paragraph. In your own words,

tell what the problem is: _____

_____

_____

write what the cause is: _____

_____

_____

tell what the effect is: _____

_____

_____

Name _____

Explaining Solutions to a Problem

Think of three possible solutions to Chris's problem as described on page 29. Write them below.

      1. Best solution: _____

      2. Next-best solution: _____

      3. Third-best solution: _____

Write a paragraph explaining the possible solutions to Chris's problem. Begin with the weakest solution and end with the best. Your paragraph should be at least seven sentences long.

_____

_____

_____

Writing to Explain copyright © 1987

Writing a Guided Problem/Solution Paragraph

Some paragraphs are written to inform people of a problem and to suggest possible solutions to the problem. For example, an editorial in a newspaper often defines a problem and proposes one or two solutions to that problem.

When writing Problem/Solution paragraphs, be sure to include each of the following steps:

1. State the problem.
2. Explain the cause of the problem.
3. Tell the result of the problem.
4. Give two or three solutions to the problem.

Directions: Complete this problem/solution paragraph by following each of the above steps.

Emerson's Problem

Emerson Robertson has a problem. He is afraid of snakes. He has been afraid of

snakes since he was five years old. When he was five, _____

_____
Since that incident, Emerson **(cause)** _____

_____
(result)

_____
There are two ways in which Emerson can overcome his fear. _____

_____
(first solution)

_____

_____
(second solution)

_____

Writing About a Current Problem

Most often we write problem/solution paragraphs about the problems we meet in our daily lives. For example, dealing with long lunch lines, overcrowded school buses, and earning pocket money are just a few of the issues we face every day.

Think of a problem you would like to see solved. Then write a problem/solution paragraph about it.

The problem I would like to write about is _____ .

Its cause is _____ .

As a result of this problem, _____

_____ .

One possible solution is _____

_____ .

I think the best solution would be _____

_____ .

Now write a problem/solution paragraph about the problem you outlined above. Begin writing on this paper and continue on another sheet if you need room.

_____

_____

_____

_____

_____

_____

_____

_____

_____

_____

Recognizing Parts in a Friendly Letter

Laura's baby sister tore up Laura's letter to her grandmother. Help Laura paste her letter back together by cutting out each section at the bottom of this page and pasting it in its proper place on the following letter form.

Address:

Date:

Greeting:

Body:

Closing:

Signature:

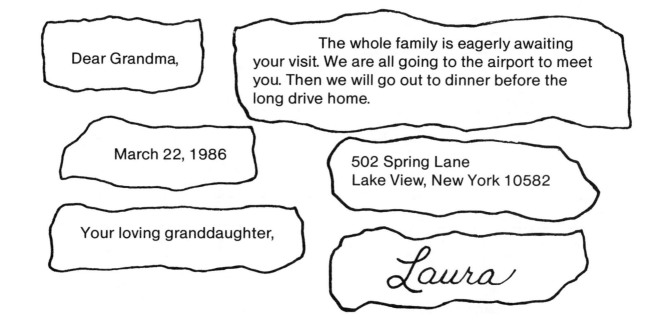

Dear Grandma,

The whole family is eagerly awaiting your visit. We are all going to the airport to meet you. Then we will go out to dinner before the long drive home.

March 22, 1986

502 Spring Lane
Lake View, New York 10582

Your loving granddaughter,

Laura

Writing a Friendly Letter

The school day for students is different in different parts of the world. The subjects studied, the number of hours and days spent in school, the daily activities, and even the style of clothes are different in each country.

Write a friendly letter to a new pen pal in China. Tell your new friend what a day in your school is like. Write your letter on the friendly letter form on this page.

Heading: _____
(Your street address)

_____
(Your city, state, and ZIP code)

_____
(Today's date)

Greeting: _____ ,

Body: _____

_____

_____

_____

_____

_____

_____

_____

_____

_____

_____

_____

_____

_____

_____

Closing: _____

Signature: _____

Writing a Letter of Advice

You are "Captain Adviser," the writer of the advice column for your class newspaper. Yesterday you received the following letter:

Dear Captain Adviser:

   I am really miserable. My parents have a new rule. I cannot watch television on school nights. Therefore, when my friends discuss programs they saw the night before, I never have anything to say. Lately, they don't even ask me to join in their conversations.
   How can I get my parents to let me watch TV? If they would just let me watch, I would be popular again.

                              Signed,
                              No TV

Step 1:   Before answering "No TV" 's letter, you must think about the problem.

1.   What two problems does "No TV" have? _____

_____

2.   Why do you think the parents made the rule? _____

_____

3.   Should "No TV" persuade the parents to change the rule? _____

4.   How? _____

5.   Could "No TV" solve the problem without changing the parents' minds? _____

_____

6.   How? _____

7.   What will you advise "No TV" to do? _____

_____

Step 2:   Write your answer to "No TV" on another sheet of paper. Be sure to use the proper friendly letter form.

Writing to Explain copyright © 1987

Writing a Letter of Explanation

Friends of your family are moving from another state to your town. Their daughter, Debbie, feels uncomfortable about living in a new town and attending a new school. Since she is your age and will be in your class at school, her mother has asked you to write her a letter explaining what your town and school are like.

Before writing your letter, think of things about your town and school that a newcomer would like to know. Then write your letter on another sheet of paper. Be sure to use the proper friendly letter form.

1. What sports and recreational activities does your town offer? _____
   _____

2. What special places are there to see? _____
   _____

3. Describe one interesting adult she will meet in your town. _____
   _____

4. Describe one or two friends who are her age and whom you think she will like.
   _____
   _____

5. Describe your school. _____
   _____

6. List three interesting projects or events you have at your school each year.
   a. _____
   b. _____
   c. _____

7. What else would you like to tell her? _____
   _____

Writing a Letter to an Author

Think of a book you really enjoyed reading. Write a letter to its author telling him or her how much you liked the book.

Before writing your letter, plan what you will say.

1. What is the title of your favorite book? _____

2. Why did you like the book so much? _____

   _____

3. Support your answer in item 2 with an example from the book. _____

   _____

   _____

   _____

4. Who was your favorite character? _____

5. Why was this character your favorite? _____

   _____

   _____

6. What incident did you enjoy the most? _____

   _____

7. Why did you enjoy it? _____

   _____

   _____

8. What would you like to ask the author about the book or about writing as a career?

   _____

   _____

   _____

Name _____

Writing a Business Letter

A business letter is different from a friendly letter. It is more formal, it has a specific purpose, and it is brief and to the point. Pretend you are moving to Pleasant Valley, California next month and that you will be entering a new school. Write a business letter to the principal of your new school. You would like information about the school you will be attending. Here are some of the things you might want to request in your letter: (1) a class schedule showing where and when your classes will meet, (2) a school calendar showing opening and closing dates of school, holidays, and special events, and (3) a copy of the dress code, if one exists. Fill in the form below as you write your letter.

Heading: _____
(Your street address)

_____
(Your city, state, and ZIP code)

_____
(Today's date)

Inside Address:

_____ , Principal
(Principal's name)

_____
(Name of school)

_____
(City, state, and ZIP code)

Greeting: _____ :

Body: _____

_____

_____

_____

_____

_____

_____

_____

_____

_____

Closing: _____

Signature: _____

Writing to Explain copyright © 1987

Writing a Business Letter to Request an Interview

Your class is involved in a project to find out what it was like to go to school sixty years ago. Your assignment is to interview Mr. Ezra Lincoln at 567 Flanders Lane. He attended your school in 1926.

Write a letter to Mr. Lincoln asking to interview him after school one day next week.

Step 1: Plan what you will say in the letter.

1. When would you like to meet with him (date, time)? _____

   _____

2. Where would you like to meet him? _____

3. Explain the purpose of your interview. _____

   _____

4. What three questions are you most interested in asking him? (If he knows them ahead of time, he can better answer them in the interview.)

   a. _____

   _____

   b. _____

   _____

   c. _____

   _____

5. Write a good closing sentence for your letter. _____

   _____

   _____

Step 2: Write your letter on a separate piece of paper. Be sure to use the correct business letter form.

Writing a Business Letter to Request Information

You have just invented a gadget that you think could make a lot of money. Your grandfather told you that the first thing an inventor should do is apply for a patent so no one else can use the idea. Write a letter to the U.S. Patent Office requesting information on filing for a patent.

Step 1: Before writing your letter, carefully plan what you will say.

1. What is the name of your invention? _____

2. What does it do? _____

3. What two questions would you like to ask about filing a patent?

      a. _____

_____

      b. _____

_____

4. Be sure to request all the forms you must fill out and file.

5. Ask for the free government pamphlet, "Filing for a Patent."

Step 2: Write a draft of the body of your letter below.

_____

_____

_____

_____

_____

_____

_____

_____

Step 3: Correct your draft for spelling and sentence errors. Then rewrite it on a separate piece of paper. Be sure to use the business letter form.

Planning a Book Report on a Biography

A biography is a story about a person's life. Famous people have many character traits we admire. Choose one famous person whose biography you have read recently and talk about a character trait you admired.

Here are some character traits you might choose:

loyalty	cheerfulness	trustworthiness	acceptance of others
honesty	shyness	sense of humor	caring for others
bravery	helpfulness	need for adventure	ability to work hard

Step 1: My famous person is _____

The character trait I admired most is _____

_____

Step 2: Think of three specific examples from the book that show this trait.

When looking for examples you may want to describe:

1. an event from the story
2. something the person said
3. something someone else said about him or her

Write your examples below.

1. _____

_____

2. _____

_____

3. _____

_____

Writing a Book Report on a Biography

Write a well-developed paragraph about the character trait of the famous person you described on page 41. Use your examples. Show how he or she demonstrated this trait in daily life.

The biography _____ by _____

_____ is a story about the life of _____

_____ . _____ had many fine character

traits, but I especially admired _____

_____ . There are many examples in the book which show this trait.

_____

_____

_____

_____

_____

_____

_____

_____

_____

_____

_____

_____

_____

_____

_____

_____

_____

_____

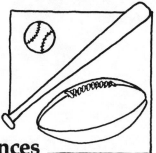

Planning a Book Report on Character Differences

Your teacher may ask you to write a book report that points out the differences between two characters in a book. Before you can begin writing this kind of book report, you must first think of all the ways the two book characters you chose are different. The contrast chart at the bottom of the page will help you plan your report. Follow the directions carefully.

Directions: **Step 1:** Think of the names of two different characters from a book you have read, and write each name in a blank at the top of the chart.

Step 2: Fill in the chart with specific differences between the two characters.

Character Contrast Chart

	Character #1 _____	Character #2 _____
Physical Appearance		
Family (size, parents, jobs, etc.)		
Activities each enjoys		
Character traits		

Writing About Character Differences

The characters in a book can be very different. Think back to the differences you outlined on the previous planning page. Think of specific actions or conversations in the book that illustrate each difference you outlined. Then write a book report explaining each difference between the two characters.

In the book _____

by _____ ,

there are two characters who are quite different from one another.

_____

_____

_____

_____

_____

_____

_____

_____

_____

_____

_____

_____

_____

_____

_____

_____

_____

_____

_____

Writing to Explain copyright © 1987

Analyzing Character Traits

We often learn what characters in short stories believe through their actions.

Name a short story you have read: _____

Who is one of the major characters? _____

What did this character value most? _____

Why was it so important to him or her? _____

_____

Which event in the story showed how important this was to the character? _____

_____

_____

Using your ideas above, write a well-developed paragraph explaining why and how this character valued what he or she did.

    In the short story _____

by _____ , _____

_____

_____

_____

_____

_____

_____

_____

_____

_____

_____

Name _____

Finding Alternative Solutions

Select a book you have read whose main character faced a problem.

Step 1: In one paragraph describe the problem and how it affected the character. Then tell how the problem was solved.

Step 2: In your second paragraph describe a different way that you think the main character could have solved that problem.

In the book _____ by _____

_____ , the main character, _____ ,

faced a difficult problem. _____

_____

_____

_____

_____

_____

_____

_____ could have solved the problem in another way.

_____

_____

_____

_____

_____

_____

_____

Comparing Eyewitness Accounts

There was a bank robbery at the Green Dollar Savings Bank yesterday at noon. The thieves took $50,000. When the police interviewed two eyewitnesses, some facts in their stories were different.

Read each eyewitness account. Underline in red pencil the facts about the robbery that are the same. Underline in black pencil, the facts that are not the same.

Eyewitness Accounts

Witness #1

I was depositing money at the teller's window when three bandits came in. They had masks on their faces and all were carrying guns. One had very black hair and the other two had blond hair. They told me to lie down on the floor and not to move. I did what they said, but I had time to notice that one man limped. He also wore cowboy boots.

I heard one man with a deep voice order the teller to put all the money in a paper bag. Then they all left, firing two shots in the air as they made their getaway. They drove away in a dark green station wagon.

Witness #2

A woman was depositing money at my window when four bank robbers entered the bank. Three came up to my window. One stood guard at the door. They had masks on their faces, but I noticed that one had black hair, and another's was light red. All of them had guns, but no shots were fired. They told the customers to lie on the floor and ordered me to fill a paper bag with money. The guy who did the talking had a low voice and walked with a limp. His boots made a strange tapping sound as he walked. As soon as I gave them the money, they left in a dark green station wagon.

Name _____

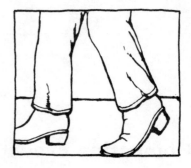

Writing Eyewitness Accounts

Using the facts in the eyewitness accounts on the preceding page, write a news report of the robbery. A good news article should include the following parts:

1. **Headline:** A title that will catch the reader's interest.
2. **Lead Sentence:** A sentence that introduces the story and answers the questions who, what, where, when, and why.
3. **Body:** The main part of the news article that gives the rest of the details. (Write the most important details first.)

Headline: _____

Lead: _____

_____

_____

_____

Body: _____

_____

_____

_____

_____

_____

_____

_____

_____

_____

_____

_____

_____

Organizing Facts for a News Feature

The playground equipment at your school needs to be replaced. Your school is having some fund-raising activities to help buy new equipment.

You have been asked to write a feature story for your local newspaper explaining the fund-raising project. Before you begin writing, think about what you want to say. Answer the questions below.

1. What is the name of your school? _____

2. What is the purpose of the fund-raising? _____

3. When will it begin and end? _____

4. Who is the person in charge? _____

5. What activities are being held to raise money? (Be sure to include when and where.)

    a. _____

_____

    b. _____

_____

    c. _____

_____

6. How much money does the school want to raise? _____

7. What playground equipment will be purchased? _____

_____

_____

Name _____

Writing a News Feature

Using the information gathered on page 49, write a feature news article explaining the fund-raising drive at your school. Be sure to mention the name of your school. Feature stories are meant to entertain as well as inform readers.

Headline: _____

Lead (Include answers 1–4): _____

_____

_____

_____

Body (Discuss activities): _____

_____

_____

_____

_____

_____

_____

_____

_____

_____

_____

_____

_____

Conclusion (Include answers 6 and 7): _____

_____

_____

_____

Organizing Facts for a Sports Article

Juanita Carlos, a sportswriter for the *City Gazette,* has been asked to write a review of the best sports event of the year. Since she cannot decide which event to write about, she is asking her readers to send her a sports article about what they think was the best sports event of the year. Send Juanita your article, but first jot down the ideas you want to write about.

1. What sports event will you write about? _____

   _____

2. When and where did it take place? _____

   _____

3. What were some of the most exciting things that happened? Jot down a brief description of three of them and tell what effect they had on the event.

   (a) _____

   _____

   _____

   _____

   _____

   (b) _____

   _____

   _____

   _____

   _____

   (c) _____

   _____

   _____

   _____

   _____

Writing a Sports Article

Now you are ready to write your sports article. Organize your notes from the previous page and begin your article with a good lead sentence. (A lead sentence tells who, what, where, when and why.) End your article by telling your reasons for selecting it as the best sports event of the year.

_____

_____

_____

_____

_____

_____

_____

_____

_____

_____

_____

_____

_____

_____

_____

_____

_____

_____

_____

_____

_____

_____

_____

Writing to Explain copyright © 1987

Planning a Restaurant Review

Congratulations on winning Metro News' Food Critic Contest. As a winner, you had dinner at the fanciest restaurant in town. Now you have been asked to write a review of your experience for the newspaper.

Before writing the review, make some notes about your dining experience.

Name of restaurant: _____

Location: _____

Date and time you were there: _____

Complete the outline below:

Foods Eaten	How Cooked (Think adjectives!) (Include sauces, seasoning, tenderness.)	How the Food Tasted
_____	_____	_____
_____	_____	_____
_____	_____	_____
_____	_____	_____
_____	_____	_____

How was the service? (Were the waitresses efficient and polite? Did you wait long?)

_____

_____

Conclusion: Did you enjoy the dinner? Would you recommend the restaurant to other

people? _____

_____

_____

_____

Writing a Restaurant Review

Now you are ready to write your restaurant review. Use the notes you made on page 53. Begin with the name and location of the restaurant. Then discuss the foods you ate and the service. Conclude with your overall impression of the place. (Be descriptive. Use strong adjectives and nouns.)

Dining Out at _____

by _____

_____

_____

_____

_____

_____

_____

_____

_____

_____

_____

_____

_____

_____

_____

_____

_____

_____

_____

_____

_____

Writing to Explain copyright © 1987

Name _____

Proofreading for Spelling Errors

Proofreading your writing is a good way to be sure you have written exactly what you wanted to say.

Directions: Proofread the following paragraphs for misspelled words.

           1. Circle each misspelled word.

           2. Write the correct spelling in the blanks below each exercise.

1.   Becuse people love to talk about monsters, some monsters are ceated just for films. For instanse, a giant ape was invented in 1933 for the movie *King Kong.* His body was made of rubber and covered with rabbit fir. Allthough the modles for some movie creatures are huge and weigh thousands of ponds, you culd hold this model in your hands.

a. _____

b. _____

c. _____

d. _____

e. _____

f. _____

g. _____

h. _____

2.   Sumtimes it is difficult to deside if monsters are real or imagninary. For example, many peple claim to have seen Bigfoot, but no real prove has ben found. Won person said he had taken a photograph of Bigfoot and his wife. The pitchur he sent too the press, however, showed only to fuzzy shapes. No one could tell if the shapes were persons, animals, or trees.

a. _____

b. _____

c. _____

d. _____

e. _____

f. _____

g. _____

h. _____

i. _____

j. _____

Proofreading for Sentence Fragments

A sentence fragment is an incomplete sentence. It is a phrase, or a group of words, that does not tell a complete thought.

Directions: Proofread each of the following exercises. If the words express a complete thought, write **"good sentence"** on the line. If the words are a phrase, and not a complete sentence, write a new sentence by adding or taking away words. The first two exercises have been done for you.

1. In China the dragon is thought to bring good luck. **good   sentence**

_____

2. If a dragon becomes angry. **If a dragon becomes angry, he could cause a flood or drought.**

3. Because dragons can bring good luck, Chinese children often fly dragon kites.

_____

4. Dragon kites that are shaped like a dragon. _____

_____

5. Since the dragon is a symbol of war in England. _____

_____

6. Their wings are small and shaped like a bat's. _____

_____

7. Dragons can fly only in short leaps. _____

_____

8. Since the lake at Loch Ness, Scotland, is almost one thousand feet deep. _____

_____

9. The Loch Ness monster, who brings thousands of people to Scotland each year.

_____

10. Although some people believe the Loch Ness monster exists. _____

_____

Writing to Explain copyright © 1987

Proofreading Newspaper Copy

Before the news is printed in the newspaper, special editors and proofreaders check it for accuracy and errors. To make their work easier, they use a set of symbols to show typesetters the changes they want to make. David's mother is an editor of a large city newspaper. She has been teaching David how to proofread newspaper copy. Study the following proofreading symbols, and then help David by proofing the news article and public service ad that will appear in his mother's paper.

Proofreading Symbols:

- ?/ means to add question mark here.
- ≡ means to capitalize the above letter.
- ⊙ means to add a period here.
- ℛ means to remove a period here.
- ⋀ means to add a comma here.
- ℛ means to remove a comma here.

News Article:

The John smith Elementary school, will be holding its spring concert in the school auditorium on january 30 at seven o'clock in the evening. the concert will be the last concert directed by Mrs. elena Green, the school's music teacher for the past thirty years Mrs. Green plans to retire at the end of this school year to her home in florida, tea and refreshments will be served after the concert during a special reception to honor mrs. Green's service to the school.

The concert program will include favorite songs from *Mary poppins* and *The Sound of music.* A poem composed and set to music by the fifth-grade class in honor of Mrs. Green will conclude the program.

Tickets are two dollars for adults and fifty cents for children under twelve they can be purchased at the door.

Public Service Ad:

Do you have a few extra hours each week The Medico memorial Hospital needs volunteers to visit with patients. volunteers are especially needed on the children's floor. Set your own hours and days call the Volunteer Service Department at the hospital.

Proofreading a Paragraph

Your friend Kelly Crabb just finished writing "My Big Fear" as an English assignment. You agree to proofread the paragraph for Kelly before it is turned in to the teacher. When proofreading, be especially watchful for:

1. run-on sentences,
2. sentence fragments, and
3. missing commas after introductory phrases and clauses.

Use the proofreading symbols you learned on the previous page.

⊙ = add a period here
≡ = capitalize the above letter
⋀ = add comma
⋋ = remove comma
⋌ = remove period

My Big Fear

Ever since I was little, I have not liked sleeping in dark rooms when I was young, I would think monsters hid under my bed. and behind my closet door. I am too big to believe in monsters now, but I still wonder about ghosts. my mom says that there are no ghosts, but she can't prove it. Ghosts are pretty slippery characters. Because they have no body. they can move in and out through keyholes. and walk through walls. I have read stories where they get your attention by slamming doors or tickling your feet. if that is all they would do. it would be fine; but in the movie *Ghostbusters*. they left green slime behind. Imagine hopping out of bed one morning and stepping into green slime! it would be truly disgusting. that is why I refuse to sleep in a dark room. Since ghosts in movies appear only in dark, spooky places I feel a light will keep ghosts and green slime out of my room.

Note: Check your work. You should have made sixteen corrections. Did you?

Writing to Explain copyright © 1987

ANSWER KEY

Unit 1: Writing Sentences

P. 1, Completing Comparison/Contrast Sentences

1. but
2. Although
3. yet
4. but
5. on the other hand
6. as
7. however
8. but
9. also
10. on the other hand

P. 2, Answers will vary.

P. 3, Completing Cause/Result Sentences

1. therefore
2. The reason
3. thus
4. Because
5. as a result
6. therefore

P. 4, Answers will vary.

Unit 2: Writing Explanatory Paragraphs

P. 5, Answers will vary.

P. 6, Writing with Examples

examples	details
dog	police work
	find people
	guide blind
pigs	TV star
chimpanzees	sign language
	spell simple words

P. 7-18, Answers will vary.

Unit 3: Writing to Compare and Contrast

P. 19-22, Answers will vary.

P. 23, Comparing and Contrasting Two Creatures

Likenesses:
1. ape-like man
2. hair on body
3. usually seen alone

Differences:

Snowman	Bigfoot
reddish-brown hair	brown or black hair
6½′ tall	over 6½′ tall
footprint 13″	footprint 16″
lives in Himalayas	lives in Pacific NW
eats goats and vegetables	eats roots, berries, leaves, meat

(Student categorization may differ slightly.)

P. 24-26, Answers will vary.

Unit 4: Writing Problem/Solution Paragraphs

P. 27-28, Answers will vary.

P. 29, Defining a Problem

problem — refuses to go on camping trip
cause — camping mishaps
effect — family unhappy

P. 30-32, Answers will vary.

Unit 5: Writing Letters

P. 33, Recognizing Parts in a Friendly Letter

Address: 502 Spring Lane, Lake View, New York 10582
Date: March 22, 1986
Greeting: Dear Grandma,
Body: The whole family . . . long drive home.
Closing: Your loving granddaughter
Signature: Laura

P. 34-40, Answers will vary

Unit 6: Writing Book Reports

P. 41-46, Answers will vary.

Unit 7: Writing Newspaper Articles

P. 47, Comparing Eyewitness Accounts

Likenesses:
wore masks
all carrying guns
black hair
customers lay down
man limped
deep voice
paper bag
dark green station wagon

Differences:

Witness # 1	Witness # 2
3 bandits	4 bandits
blond hair	light red hair
2 shots fired	no shots fired

P. 48-54, Answers will vary

Unit 8: Proofreading

P. 55, Proofreading for Spelling Errors

1.
a. Because
b. created
c. instance
d. fur
e. Although
f. models
g. pounds
h. could

2.
a. Sometimes
b. decide
c. imaginary
d. people
e. proof
f. been
g. One
h. picture
i. to
j. two

P. 56, Proofreading for Sentence Fragments

3. Good sentence
4. Sentence fragment
5. Sentence fragment
6. Good sentence
7. Good sentence
8. Sentence fragment
9. Sentence fragment
10. Sentence fragment

ANSWER KEY (Continued)

P. 57, Proofreading Newspaper Copy

News Article:

The John smith Elementary school will be holding its spring concert in the school auditorium on january 30 at seven o'clock in the evening. the concert will be the last concert directed by Mrs. elena Green, the school's music teacher for the past thirty years Mrs. Green plans to retire at the end of this school year to her home in florida, tea and refreshments will be served after the concert during a special reception to honor mrs. Green's service to the school.

The concert program will include favorite songs from *Mary poppins* and *The Sound of music.* A poem composed and set to music by the fifth-grade class in honor of Mrs. Green will conclude the program.

Tickets are two dollars for adults and fifty cents for children under twelve they can be purchased at the door.

Public Service Ad:

Do you have a few extra hours each week? The Medico memorial Hospital needs volunteers to visit with patients. volunteers are especially needed on the children's floor. Set your own hours and days call the Volunteer Service Department at the hospital.

P. 58, Proofreading a Paragraph

My Big Fear

Ever since I was little, I have not liked sleeping in dark rooms when I was young, I would think monsters hid under my bed and behind my closet door. I am too big to believe in monsters now, but I still wonder about ghosts. my mom says that there are no ghosts, but she can't prove it. Ghosts are pretty slippery characters. Because they have no body they can move in and out through keyholes and walk through walls. I have read stories where they get your attention by slamming doors or tickling your feet. if that is all they would do it would be fine; but in the movie *Ghostbusters* they left green slime behind. Imagine hopping out of bed one morning and stepping into green slime! it would be truly disgusting that is why I refuse to sleep in a dark room. Since ghosts in movies appear only in dark, spooky places I feel a light will keep ghosts and green slime out of my room.